William Bevill
The Razor Graveyard

A Puppy Mummy/ Dr Benway Publication
Tucson, Arizona, 85745

http://www.lulu.com/williambevill

First edition, 2007

ISBN 978-0-6151-5037-6

Introduction

Thank you for reading my book. It is with great pride that I release this collection of poems/thoughts/dreams. Many of these have been written as far back as 1994, so the book is a long time coming. I have divided it into two sections. The first is "The Razor Graveyard" a collection of my more recent works. It is concluded with a very long collection of poems lumped together as one giant "Razor Graveyard" poem.

The second part is "The Grand Unified Theory of The Ball" which I published in 2006.

What is a Razor Graveyard and a Grand Unified Theory of a Ball? Dreams and creativity and pure madness. Sometimes, it's better to just enjoy the words and hopefully be mildly amused.

November 2006 **William Bevill**

Contents

The Grand Unified Theory of the Ball

I
The Razor Graveyard

Just Desserts

The old ladies sit on their seats inside a hollowed out oak tree
deep in a vast forest of no light, no return.

The seats they sit upon creak.

Old seats, covered with tough leather, leather that is beginning to
peel and crack.

Centuries of odd ornaments are lost inside the wooden seats, long forgotten.
The haggard old lady, as old as the oak tree she lives in, stares into a
giant steel pot.

The pot is a faded shade of black that not been cleaned for many decades.
It sits upon a roaring red hot fire. A liquid substance of blood is
cooking inside.

The lady next to her laughs as she stirs the pot. Red blood boils and screams,
calling for someone that is no longer there.
It is alive.

They laugh out loud, happy with the day's work, and look at each other with
great love.

The liquid is not quite done.

The ladies add their secret recipes to the brew, and it pleases them greatly.

The sound of their laughter spreads far into the forest.

The mix is cooled and eaten under a dim and pale light of yellow.

The ladies cackle, and eat their raspberry Jell-O.

City Suicide

There cannot be silence in a city
it is inconceivable for such a phenomenon
which makes this particular moment
unique and unsettling
my stomach got queasy just now
time seems to have frozen
even in city silence
I always hear a hum of sorts
some nuclear energy making snorts
or a car racing to rush into a red light
but now, none of that
I am haunted at the droll nothingness
a vast landscape haunted
by complete tone deafness
I'd like to photograph it
take a picture of silence
in the city.

Animal Companion Program

Companionship of animals is lonely
creatures who won't verbally communicate
but are never at a loss for words
they have reactions to my movements and follow my actions
nothing beats peering into the eye of a pet and seeing them gaze back
in expectance of a little bit of attention or a treat
in a home of solitude
and great disappointments
there is a need for the sounds the animals make
as they interact and go their way
without their presence
I think I would feel absolute isolation.

Co-Op

I gazed at the girl in the health food store
energy surging through me
kind of like one of the crystals hanging near the organic pomegranates
she radiated with eco-friendly glistening scents similar to that of a frisky otter
diluted pupils in her eyes expanding
long unwashed hair tied with a Grateful Dead ribbon.
I fell for her with the intensity of a soy bean pancake, and she didn't even see my eyes

I imagined a chance encounter there and then at the health food store
just me and her and the produce fruit section and perhaps some animal cruelty free lotion.
There would be a kind of energetic force that happens when two cosmic beings united and copulate.

I put a zucchini against her underwear and said,
        "Wow, what nice weather outside."
I could almost taste the beeswax lip-gloss dripping from her mouth
her feet wiggled inside lovely brown, faded suede sandals
those unwashed toes inching toward my legs in dramatic pursuit.
Hairy legs rubbing against mine like matchsticks.
She pushed me into the aromatherapy display in blind lust and bit my ear.
        "Ow!" I said.

True romance comes in a cloth shopping bag.

Theater Dream

There is something erotic about the matinee show
forcing our way across the gates to discover cinema magic
the front entrance to the theater blocked
people having abandoned the way of life
years ago
something imminent, something horrific
they fled with little time to spare
the complex was not safe
death or slow suffocation was coming to them
and the theater was shut, doomed
memories of entire families sealed inside, doors barred, fences erected
the nucleus entombed
this little place in the outskirts of town went ignored
until curious folk immerged, eager to learn its secrets
they found holes in the fence ignored
and went in
with force
he waited, curious, scared
staring down the hallway of a dark corridor
and they returned with news of its wonders and curiosities
to them this was an empty building to party and drink and screw around in
but this theater
was a shrine
to him
a monument to time standing still
a society forgotten, left clinging with the elderly,
a dying memory
he ran in and saw the giant movie screen, ripped and scarred from time,
hanging over a stage precariously
eroded floorboards looked creaky and worn and dangerous to thread upon
he went up a hallway to the left, jumping over halls on the floor, to view the
projection room
an empty window that once housed a thousand silent silver cinema films.

Midget

I'm in love
so in love
with a dwarf.
My love stands three feet high
but has a big smile
I'm head over high feels for my midget
who will stand on her toes
my love is like a pint sized milk carton
but you can't deny a tiny heart
that beats all day with love.
I love my midget's hair
I love saying to her
"Honey, it's a sunset, come stand on a chair."
I cook all her meals
because she can't reach the stove
and I marvel at her height in stilettos
I rescued her from life as a circus clown
gave her confidence, hope, and platform shoes
even as three-year olds knock her down.
My love is for a dwarf
a pint sized Rice-A-Roni bundle of love
my midget and me fly low.

The City

Sniffing fish on a pungent wharf station
she brought him another hat
one more from a salvation store.
His own collection
he did not know how much the little pile she brought him would mean
he lived in a place underneath the city with them
yet it seemed so high above the hills
overlooking magic caverns
and a restaurant serving spicy peppers
storms flow on.
An eastside mortuary faces the street
a house on hollow's eve has run out of candy
and the only thing they can pass out are handfuls of pennies and nickels
the children gobble them up with eager greed
down the road is the carnival store giving away
glasses made in 3-D, and I sit close and stare
at the shark bites overlapping the silver screen.
Felt an electricity surge through
a black child lives in university housing
the only one in town playing the Disney Channel
I went there
gave up action figures to a boy to see it
I didn't mind if they were returned with the hands chewed off.
He remembers his first bicycle, from the first every Christmas
never again in a million years would anything top that
he found recycled gadgets and wrapped them under the tree
looks upon the growing trees that expand outside the parking lot
and that empty union full of food for starving people- yummy prunes.
She grabs my hand and leads me
into a building full of relics born so many years before me
not thinking about what lies ahead
escaped onto the street with the warning of explosions impending
looked across at a plate glass full of amazing confectionaries
that would become the little haven, the place he would associate forever
with her
shared over a powdered jelly donut

don't you
remember
we went there again and again
sharing donuts and juice and milk
in such a little city
an entire giant civilization flowed
where overpowering trees bulged over the stream
and crosswalks and walkways twisted and turned in a variety of directions
even as thunder storms rumbled on
cold drops wetting his ecstatic face, he rode onward
feet on metal
the pedals of the bike eagerly racing forward
antique stores, burger joints, chocolate fairy tale lands full of queens
a train embedded in marble rock with dozens of trapped victims lost
inside forever
a hospital on a hill fenced in with broken down windows and abandoned
gurneys
he breathed a shallow breath
and remembered the strangest things
of a time when everything seemed extraordinary
when childhood eternity stood still and all was vibrant
I block out the memory
of sitting in a backseat watching it all go away
seeing the little girl from across the street waving farewell to him
he thought about jumping off that bridge
just to stay
to get his feet wet in the moss drenched rocky waters
and wait for the flood to come
& carry him down stream for miles
seeing underground tunnels for exploration
formed the city in my head
and now I see where it built me
and I follow it
there.

The Violent Raping of a Greasy Plumber

The criminal act of lovemaking and coital pleasure
had ended abruptly like a mummy encased to the tomb
sealed in the room of the mothball kings
around midnight
two star crossed lovers jumped off a bridge
into the freezing rippling water of the creek,
its wet coat shined blue of reflections cast from unseen neon lamps
that burned on the front porch of an old fashioned wicker built pub
soggy and moist vines in the narrow swamps
there was the dull, damp sound of a shovel smashing
over the head of a greasy plumber, the repeated bashings on his
swollen forehead
resembling that of a dull sword cutting away at a La-Z-Boy
his excrement coated hands tried in desperation to grip the pipes
of the repair job he was working on
and the pipe cracked off, grubby fingers clutching
his wrist snapped, the bone crackling as easily as a matchstick.
The evening matinee show comes to a close
three gorgeous ladies of the night
meander out the exit doors
chattering loudly and spreading lipstick lazily
in dramatic sweeps of gold and amber hues
none of these oblivious skanks
could see the boy hiding in the high hedge
his eyes sparkling as the theater lights struck their glitter
splashed faces
and he ran out across the sidewalk and screamed
one of the girls dabbed on heavy eyeliner until her eyes looked beaten
as though a jealous lover had welcomed her home
and his hands grabbed clumsily at her stockings,
pulling & gnawing at them with his teeth
and she enjoyed hardcore nausea sweeping her body
her aching hands felt inside his raincoat to find out what he had
to see if he was pure
to learn if all that boasting had been real
or was that just dialogue excellently executed in a poor motion picture
the greasy plumber bled slowly to death

the beating mass of his grey and pink fleshy brain squirted the
occasional shot of unnecessarily thick red blood
like ketchup from a violently shaken bottle.

She would enter the bathroom later that evening
swearing in sailor style
seeking a towel and trekking her feet through cold, damp floors
and mushy carpets
she would turn on the lights and wonder what she had stepped in
this brilliant plasma of a former plumber was matted in clumps of
flesh and hair
and she would wonder what color she had painted her toes that
morning.

Love, Love, Love!

My love grows each passing day for you until I resemble
an oak tree spreading its branches
which in a way fits me physically
since I got bigger and fatter when we got together.
on my diet of potato chips and raspberry Seltzer water
girth rules
embrace my trunk.
My love for you is like Romeo and Juliet
but I probably wouldn't swallow poison
even if you did
but I'd be touched by your gesture, quite honestly
and in my arms as you breathed your last gasps
I'd probably ask
"Can I go out with other girls?"
Love, love it's great! Love, I love to be in love!
It's a great thing. To be in love is pure love.
Why reminisce when you should feel bliss,
it's a great day for loving, so be in love!
I love the way my heart faints when I see my sweetie
That is how in love I am! You dance and you sing and you play.
Acting like giddy school children at recess, there is definitely no
excess, when it comes to love!
You'll feel jubilation as you skip
a beat to meet your sweetheart.
Look, even the weather channel forecasted great weather
it's a great day to be in love!
If I could be in love with the love I have
there would be too much joy and pleasure
sweeping the land
I'd be a contagious love bug and the moment people saw me
they'd forget about their worries and say
"Hey! I'm in love today! And tomorrow, and maybe even yesterday!"
So what are you waiting for
If you don't act now, you'll be missing another minute of love
I love you, love!
10% chance of sun
90% chance of rain
100% of love!

Moon Walk

The fresh linen socks on a couch
are most satisfying comfort
lateness of an undetermined hour
after distractions of the traffic hiss halts
and perhaps somewhere out there
a person just turned 21
I hike up my pants and yearn for a cigar
then wink at the moon
illuminated path to the rocky trail
sort of a monochrome haze, a newsprint enviroscape.
I like knowing the only timecard here is the one due
as the sun rises.

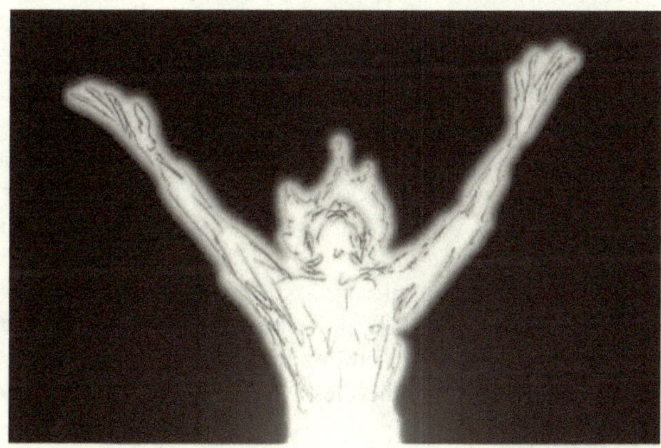

Blaqueheart

The ? Mark

There is violation
for you to feel pleasure and pain
or feel love for
a boy, a lover
a friend
spending his time overnight 1-5 days in jail
and released for you to taste him again
enjoyment inside a tightly packed seat
viewing passing roads and green bushes
hiding the fading wood signs and frogs
just a few things make me satisfied
I pick hairs off my legs in protest
cruising a few hundred miles across brick top
with sporty low cruisers speeding by in mythological fashion
like modern day knights and kings in an urban pub
serving frothy fresh cider and fermented ale to weary travelers
with worn engines and a thirst for proper tomatoes and beans for
breakfast
the ultimate meal of the day
not enough to serve this face
I'm wanting a bit more, seeking any handout, a freebie
Or a warm kettle in the morning
a chance to sneak away & buy the t-shirt of a grunge band
he tries to hide
ready to explode in steaming passion
and a shriek erupting from the closet and running to the aid
of a mother catching falling objects off the top shelf
she was the first person he would call in the case of an emergency, a
tropical storm or an urban boy following him on the street
or knocking balls weirdly on the course with golf holes that hooked
left onto the freeway.
He stares down into a glass filled with darkened beverage
smelling faintly like urbanization and carbonation and advertising
with hollowed chunks of chilled ice floating
pushing down, bobbing helplessly, wishing to be somewhere else,
anywhere else
and his mouth gulps greedily forward
cheeks gulping, enveloping, absorbing and overtaking

a stream of desire in one glass, a box hidden under the sink, but
known to everyone in the household
just not in use by anyone else
a dry escape to get away
the ridiculous nature of the boy upstairs that lived and crawled silently
a creature stirring in the night with a desire of gazing at the smear of
light cracking into the skylight
the one he dreamt of at night
crawling via the bathroom
push his way in
would they catch him there?
Would anyone?

Who Did Who

Barney was a licker
Johnny enjoyed his liquor
Fred smoked crack
Lionel sold him smack
Wilma was a whore
Gina heard her snore
Betty had a bong
Timmy had no dong
Mike was a flunky
Duke was just a junkie
Carol was on meth
She smoked it with Seth
Marsha enjoyed anal
Richard was anal
Cindy liked getting high
Joy showed her how to fly
Greg used his gun
One legged Jake had to run
Jan was a slut
Seth did her butt
Bobby had a hobby
Uncle Fred was his hobby
Oliver lost his eyesight
to Ned at a bar fight
Peter got into Germans
Deiter got into Peter.

The Pen Is Dead

The pen is dead
the pen has no more ink
because the pen is dead
I won't write anymore
cause the pen has died
it is really simple
the reason I can't write
is that the pen is dead
stupid!
It used to have ink
but now it does not
so the pen is dead
(It was a very good pen, a pilot P-700.
Now the pen is dead. That's all I have left to say).

A Reluctant Farewell

Candy colored and lucid pink
you are so vibrant
full of life
mashed between my pillows
I will make you my wife
toss your hair up
and move right in
so clean and beautiful
you are the best thing since sin.
Why can't you be more than this
face the tumble of the storm
people like you are the reason I am in disgust
I cannot open my eyes and miss you in my view
I'd rather walk on daggers than miss out
it is just a matter of time
the day I erode
you are exactly like me, a facsimile on a weathered and
beaten copy machine

Windowsills

I'm riding in the backseat of a strange car
I could probably get a clue
we are stuck behind a camel and I don't think we will go far
yet I don't really care about bursting barns or backyards igniting
in flames
but the only thing that matters is safety
so I'll take this chance to duck down, and pretend to pray
I work on a novel, yet all I hear anyone say
is what a shame we won't go to the circus this year
but none of that really matters since lateness is the hour
I'm mindful of your privacy
no inhibitions to get ahead, you have to scream
hiding behind a mirror to fight off another image to tease
built like a machine
but I don't know what functions they serve
I could be trapped underneath a moving van
or propped inside the outlet stores working as a mannequin.
It is rather peculiar
this mirage of sunsets
inside the clam baked oven
and the frame shall portray a stain of a fragmented memory
upon a funny mirror
the kind of panic I'll get
leaves me in a hassle, a dried mouth and a painful collar on the neck
I worry about sin colored rainbows and dried raisins resting on
window stills
devoured
I overcompensate
because I want to reincarnate
with sensual needs my eye is on the play at hand
can't they go and be on their way?
And if I go out in a fiery red crash I have so much left I want to tell
fond farewells left uncompleted, but at least I would not disappear
with time
well then they asked, who is your favorite? And in no way could I
reply.
I melt on the windowsill
this is all I can manage to say.

Baby Bouncing

Warm wild child cozy in his cot
he cuddles up and coos in a fetal ball
bouncy, bubbly little creature
so playfully innocent of its surroundings
a narcissistic tyke that you can't help but like
even when you want to twist its ungrateful neck
fun baby rolls in the sun
dribble, drop spittle, oh the chores
baby has gone
and unloaded in his drawers!

Magic Button

You have a magic button
to press and go
when we touch one another's button
things start to happen.
There was that memorable first time
your eyes lit up
by the glow of the alarm clock
and hearing the distant humming of old creaky pipes
and we touched buttons
yours made you go wild
and we acted out a theater play
like two people
without a script in mind

Loving a Smurf

She's blue! She's blue!
I'm in love with you! With you!
I want to marry a smurf
She's bad ass and she's blue
with all my heart I know it's true
come on over and see
visit her and me on the turf
it's with Smurfette I must forever be
in love with a smurf, that's me!
With her bright blue tones and
golden lock pigtails
she sends shocks and signals
from my toes to my entrails.
She lights up my life
in an aqua kinda way
be still my beating heart
that beats in unison with both of yours.

Free to Bee

The hearth that will warm the man
the fruit on a platter is dinner
the sun on his feet makes him gladder
on the run
looking far
he jumps the gun
the tree the rabbit will see
the flea the rabbit wishes to be
a bee the rabbit wants honey
a key, the rabbit sees thirty-three
with glee the rabbit is free
a knee, the rabbit can flee
some tea
the rabbit will see
the tree
the flea
the bee
a key
with glee, floating at sea, counting to thirty-three,
he will be free.

Everything

I have become rock & roll
I am the washboard left sitting
behind a crate in your backyard
I have become the wilting flower
ready to drop & tired of waiting for the parade
I'm a child ignored, discouraged
a wish you made
I'm a kitten stranded, too ugly to be petted
and too tame to survive
I'm a hundred thousand raindrops
falling at your feet in the blink of an eye
I'm a soggy pair of shoes that met when they were dry
I became all these things. And more.

My DVD is Stuck

My DVD is stuck on the menu mode
and it won't do anything else because
I lost the remote
and my DVD is stuck there
I can't make it play.
It's taunting me with previews of the movie I want to see
but I can't find that fucking remote anywhere
and none of the buttons on the player will make it go.
I'm not sure what to do
I'm so very sad
The DVD is stuck on the menu option
I've been listening to the same music for about half
an hour
just out of grasp of so many special features and chapters
and cool foreign subtitles
What ever will I do?
I guess I'll turn on the VCR.

$.99 Cent Store

I just spent five dollars
at the .99 cent store
I am infatuated with the $.99 cent store
no, I am seriously goddamn infatuated with the .99 cent store!
I have never had more quality time in my life than at this place
It is utopia
around me, surrounding me
are $.99 cent items
everywhere.
Tools
toys
books
kitchen gadgets
even candy bars?
Dear lord, I can buy everything here!
I fell in love with a girl at the $.99 cent store
fell in love with her today without a discount sale to be found
I will go home and I will cry over her and watch Donahue
and air out my shoes
she is so pretty and she sells things that cost only $.99 cents
destiny is going to happen and she doesn't even know it
since she's ringing up patron's at the cash register a buck an item
someone just bought lipstick, band aids, fertilizer, a trash can, bleach and imitation cologne of Elizabeth Taylor
and my god! They only paid $.99 cents for each!
With broom in hand, two packages of gummy bears, an air freshener and plastic flowers
I approach the girl of my dreams, the penny pincher, the discount queen of the world
with dollar bills held firmly in hand
those which I spared from spending at the stripper show last night
I will firmly thrust them into her brittle white trash fingers
she is all my mine
we will have fun tonight
for just $2.99.

Deirfgeis & Yor

People ask me why I avoid you but I can't say
I am paranoid and obsessive and I stand in the water and freak at the rust
whenever I walk into a bar or a shop or a club I feel like they are
all watching
so I turn the channel and think about the animals
slide into a water fall
I feel a whole lot safer in the Siegfried & Roy gardens

Rotating Boy

He moves around a lot
because he is a rotating boy
he does not have a home and he never owned a garden gnome
he is a rotating boy
neighborhoods are for changing and rearranging and musical chairs
onwards young child, march! Push! Forward, tally ho!
Viva la France, he yells
as he relocates to a bungalow
life is good for the rotating boy
when you listen to him talking
you realize he has no voice of his own
he is an expert mimicker
a boy with no personality of his own
he left it packed in the moving van
the rotating and relocatable boy
a misogynist at heart, he loathes the population at large
and yet has these crazy freaky yearnings
hold 'em up partners, you've crossed into Texas territory, remove yer holster
yee haw!

Skillet

I dip bricks over an iron skillet
and sizzle the hell out of a verbal argument from a crazy clerk
whirling fans on a California mountaintop
remind me of a dairy that brings home to us
the misery of being a clown
dressed only in black and white and throat lozenges
and manic high tone helium laughs.
I burst a bubble of gas. It's no laughing matter. Haw haw.
The dent
I escape for the new creation
and my empty pockets beg for change
fern trees in the valley
the missiles guide me there.

Fang

Wild jagged teeth
fangs fucking in and out
farming sheep pigs
        goose bumps
blood roasted lame & crippled
thirsty pangs of misery.
Crafty, cruel and demanding
girls in heat, feeling, sucking
calm cool release
        I'm burning.
Bite down, shut up your radio.

Garden of Place

Carpets cool and copulating
mating during a hot summer day
as skin melts to the dashboard
awash in guilt and ready
to choose the first who wakes
I am the best
I am the least flea bitten
and you
place second always
no veteran, a success
caught escaping in the line of fire
multitudes of twirling crosses.
Dominant apes
chew on their bananas of gain.

Sofia Blue

Drinking as an Artform

I like to drink and I like to joke about it
and the truth is I can really drink it with the best of them
and joke about it the next day while nursing a hangover.
I'm often asked where I went drinking the night before
only as far as my living room, says I
pouring glass after glass of sweet lovely ice
dreaming and fantasizing about mouthfuls
of refreshing tonic.
The home drinker is a specialized art
an alcoholic of the isolated variety
one must be very sneaky about staying home and
avoiding social engagements
the experienced drinker knows how expensive going to
town is.
There should be a guide to drinking at home
the term "economical drinker" is exciting
in this day of social correctness.

I'm Blowing Apart Glass in the World

Million dollar winning Playboy aristocratic monkey men swab each other tenderly with cue sticks
spreading cholera and hydrogen peroxide
seems one of them has a fetish for baking soda and rubs it on his gums at night in the dark before the mirror shuts down.
A bloody formerly crucified wall street lawyer in a George Foreman business suit pats his boss on the back and jabs him in the spine again with a steak knife from a set he ordered on TV that came with a free chopping board, which he uses in the kitchen for lettuce and cucumbers.
He seems a little bored, so this makes the evening pass without the use of a game of Yahtzee or Twister.

Obsessed with Frank Sinatra, a team of homeless ladies run down the street with plastic bags held high, hoping the wind will carry them away.

A new age hippie named Bart sells organic tofu and bean sprouts to lonely and quiet customers in a grocery store, all of them acting
shady and disturbed, like they were buying pornographic movies from a 24-hour sex shop. Bart watches them file by one by one and secretly keeps his eye on a man, whom he has a little crush on. He will bite his lip and finger the environmentally aware shopping bag for comfort, followed by tofu flavored gum drops.

Two guys guzzle red wine from a bottle and play Jenga, watching the hours roll by, sad, lonely, depraved, hungry, and one of them missing somebody terribly. The wine gets things a little crazy and...

A man goes running outside in 40 degree weather wearing shorts and a t-shirt, his beer belly starting to hang out, and frosty winds bite his throat as he races himself. The girl at the desk will be waiting, not for him, not for anyone or anything, and she'll laugh at him.

Menthol cigarettes smoked on snow covered benches.

A pretty young girl leaves her room with mascara smeared around her eyes, fresh from a nap, wanting a cigarette, dreading going to A.A again. She'll probably just go home that weekend and screw it all.

Boy walks up the hill and his backpack falls open and papers and notebooks fall out, flying off in the wind, and he breaks down crying and everyone watches with disinterest.

Green, the unlucky color of the spectrum, is quickly removed. Then he sees it in a motion picture and realizes there is validation and maybe he won't have to cure it after all. And the motion picture becomes his life.

Watched a reality show, drank from a glass bottle poured into a thirst buster cup. Repeated again.

TV for the Dead

Zombie television is a channel relentlessly turned on
fuzzy in nature with gray and white dots and gravestones in color
heartless bodies rise to pass on their wisdom and knowledge to the elders
and in the meantime, eating and shredding flesh by means of soft molars

Funeral Clowns

Godzillas and gods create a bubble environment
a happy fun place with smiles, balloons, and funeral clowns
they come from all over, to merry up the final rites of the soon to be buried.
Interior: funeral home, filled with grieving and devastated family and friends
playing droning sad organ music as tears and sobs mingle with misery
Enter: Funeral Clowns!
They run in and do somersaults and bounce and yell and laugh and make things all better
look out for them, they make appearances at any juncture at almost no cost
beaming and happy faces with bright red noses, honking horns and squirting flowers
they come to celebrate and cheer everyone up
in a moment of the clown's work,
the deceased body in the casket suddenly has giant colorful flipper shoes
oh what joy
funeral clowns are here to hug those sobbing family members grieving from a sudden death
and make a quarter disappear from your ear
When death has struck, pick up the phone, dial, leave a message, and you'll soon have laughter and merriment
whether it's today, tomorrow, or 3-4 weeks on the life support machine, funeral clowns are there
maybe they can even come to your own funeral if you plan ahead!

All Star Sociopath

I'm crazy enough to send your ass to the pet hotel
or drink a giant glass of cherry syrup flavored brandy with a dash of sangria
and gulp children's cough medicine for taste
nobody cares if this is where it ends
since I'm just exhibiting dictator-like qualities in a society of the bland
I wonder if being kind of an all-star psychopath is a good thing
because it sure is great for my diet by sticking my nose in my business
and I think really hard about thick candy created in a factory and the sun
I get really hard
when I get glue on my hands
I love the look and smell of fizzling charcoal and embers wilting in the air
oh gee, I have a lot of fun
at the sight of a basement full of kinky queens and queer kings
I used my influence in the right places to show them all how crazy I am and
to buy up plots of land in useless places so I can roll around in the sand
for a tan
more problems could be solved by drinking grapefruit juice or chewing on
rubber pencils
come with me to the grocery store and we'll split the groceries in half
one half of the popular toilet seat and the other into my dusty, dank
water closet
I'm excited by colorful traffic lights at midnight
Jesus saves
I could get really involved and make a difference to the rest of the world
but when you have as much as I do there just isn't much room to care
come with me and play and that'll be okay with the boy and his marble face
and a gluttony of bills in his shirt pocket ready to soak in
she will comatose in an overdose of sinful playfulness
the other end of a dark underground channel
an emerald river guzzles along
sucking on word captions captured from television
we entered the grassy and moss swollen entrance of a Mexican pyramid
and felt purified within as the factory tubes pump out clumps of black
smoke.

Playpen of Dr. Death
(Pirates who drink the people's blood but don't smell the stench)

Organic children were bred in the laboratory of Dr. Death
he smoked cigars and inhaled his own smelly farts like crack cocaine
his laughter was harsh as a hyena
long since abandoning food he now turned only to tonic water
as his supplement
a revered man, not long sought after, with bulbous cheeks that cackled
the greatest experiment of all time had gone all wrong,
"The Experiment"
something horrible had not proceeded as planned
and nobody would choose to admit fault for it except Dr. Death
who cut out his own tongue to try and clone a new one.
And he know his mistake meant nothing would ever go right again
there was a terrible silence, a nasty darkness
a slice into the body, cutting like homogenized knives into skin and yielding
milk
proactive poodles
the field was full of rotting babies
and horny corpses
swarming with leeches, sucking away
eyes of a cat
you could see him in the dark
waiting to pray upon
the gorgeous ones.

Peace Carpet (with Leon Ortega)

You are a celebrity and you know it so
a rock star wearing a manhole cover blasting an electric flute
rocking out and chopping down bonsai trees
feeling the sting of electric eels
getting real high, yeah
I'll follow you across the railroad tracks
and we'll go down to Mexico and splash happily into the salty sea
together you and me we'll live in a peace carpet
        baby baby
roll that mother up, blaze it, and get out of your coffin
pack sandwiches and roll a few smokes since we're taking a flight
going to Venice and Rome via the peace carpet
watching log cabins burn down
smoke stacks casting off peppermint candies
and we inhale it and get high baby cause we're up in the sky
with a kite knitted by a crazy mother addicted to Jazz
we stood in the sun, thinking about old times sakes
the restaurant by the street was still there
nothing had changed
I'd landed in a new, different, world
and all of this seems ridiculous bouncing off 2 x 2 's of pine wood
do you remember when you donned a superhero shirt and sunk
in the mud
thigh high boots scrambling
fearful of loose barking dogs cruising the street wearing sunglasses
        Peace Carpet
found heaven now
point a finger on the map to go
anywhere, just stick it somewhere, we can find the way if I don't know
feel wind whipping across your face
and tossing your hair back
going flying, oh yes, going flying, in the peace carpet.

Arts & Crafts Suicide

My mother died
and I alternate between coping well
and inventing exciting ways to kill myself creatively.
Expressing thyself with body cuts
because we all seek to show our individuality in one way or another.
I've thought of Molotov cocktails and hungry piranhas and sandwiches fixed with butter and arsenic
there are so many exciting ways one could die, using many chemicals on any shelf, with or without lighter fluid
tons of things out there and all I have to do is inject, sniff or lick or
suck a toad.
I've spend afternoons reading the letters of the dead
thinking about what I would compose were it my time
what would be my final letter
my final contribution to the world, whatever could be said
a dedication for the ages.
Will I be remembered for a book or two
or will they think about how I overdosed from eating a bucket of glue?
I want to pack up my car with gallons of gas and six sticks of dynamite
head somewhere pretty, see a sunset and drive off a cliff
and as I fly through the air I'll think, "Damn, this dynamite won't work, I don't have a light!"

Fantastic Whispers

Traffic was insane
I drove you away
and I pushed to keep you out
you made every effort to come in
while I stood and said no
cried myself hoarse
in a car on a nothing kind of ride
I have but the memories
and a promise to stay there in the spirit of you
maybe now we'll be stronger
than I ever let us be the last many years
just as I was coming around
like you knew I would and you told others
you saw it coming
you went out of my life
left me all alone
and the best I can do is stay strong
I would have given anything not to see you in pain
how amazing was it though
in those final days
we could see each other and look at each other
and knew what this meant
if there was anyone for you
I knew it was me and I always know it was me
and you left that trust in me
made up for all those times I pushed us away
we saw it there that first night of the end
allowing the passage, accepting it all
I didn't let you down
to the final confused months of a twisted time
we took our turns and journeys
and found our own little way and in the end brought us together
in something so meaningless the way you had to go
so short and so cruel and so unfair
but I know what you did for me was another challenge
and you garden and watch and curl up on the couch with the final episodes
waiting to see where I go and what I do.

Retirement Party for a Dead Person

The solemness of the office party was spoiled by the death of a co-worker
the crowded room was filled with people feigning interest
sorta like a planned office party of immodesty and fakeness and people who'd rather be at home
but are showing up to say goodbye to you, because you're gonna die
and all the people were really feeling a huge inconvenience
by having to act like they cared to see you and invest in flowers
and show up and sign a guest book expressing their greetings
sit around and talk about work and laugh, thinking about getting drunk
& enjoyable little awkward silences
While skirting the topic of you croaking soon, life goes on
so stand around the water cooler pretending to give a fuck.
For someone who has a few weeks of life and pain
it's pretty amusing really
seeing people who'll be, like, so over this in a couple of days or so
hey, wander in and get a tour!
on your left, dying person
on your right, look at this beautiful bookshelf!
Oh, hey how're things at work
aw that's too bad
oh really
wow that mush food looks nasty
(Retirement party for a dead person in action here)
it's amazing how much weight someone loses when they're dead, you know?
What a great garden this is
did ya hear about that promotion?
I know it'll mean a whole lot to you after you die, and stuff, to know what we're telling you
what a great bed sheets you have
"I haven't seen you this happy in years"
you probably want to be alone, but we're self servicing!
Oh, retirement parties for a dead person, what a gas
gather around the toxic water cooler
take a sip of the deceased
mourn for the morgue
emails for the dead person! Express death in callous electronic print!
Joke and laugh and cough a lot and scream in pain on the tour
that is a retirement party for the dead, in slow motion action.

Sofia Blue

The Razor Graveyard

You might laugh at me
but that was deserved
throats explore tongues
mingling with hyperactive frenzied arms and legs
you should have known it was going to work
steaming your glasses thick
till sweat pours down like deep circles
stinging my eyes
you might laugh and hope you deserve it
pouncing ourselves into a pretzel shaped formation
let me salute the flag from my hips on up.

Little soldiers from Babylon
are beautiful and won't hesitate
to spread joy across the globe
they go with the flow
see the poem aside your head
drag the razor, scream and cry
go get wasted
spend the next decade tasting
swallow but don't spit
find the trail marker at the end of the canyon
with arrow signs facing forward toward the graveyard
the little children put the ball in the hoop
more than the other team
the faith can be stuck in the mailbox and hand delivered by a guy in a coat
I've been waiting for you to arrive
with a precious document explaining how to perform the surgery
and all the energy of a hung-over doctor with scalpel in hand
time to get talking and wait for a lit moon
to choose the best headstone
and we'll lay across the grave and smear fake blood on our throats
and hope for guys with flashlights to show up
to see the hollow eyes on my face
that are inviting us like the devil on a bed.
I plan to stay one step ahead
even with a courtyard of razors slicing through skin
as easily as hot knives in buttered flapjacks
I'm strong as an ox but pumped full of energy pills
ready to pull bulls
this life was never wrong
all I can do is switch on the blinkers, gun the gas and drive right ahead
drag the razor and scream and cry and drop the faith behind
the open sores on your lips burn and need attending to
so get off your duff and quit wasting
I'll never head back to the razor graveyard, that's for sure
spent too much time wasting and waiting for some answer
wishing life was like a song
great at the beginning and awesome at the end
but thinking the bridge is a bit of a letdown
lowering myself away to the grave and swallowing the sores that'll let me
ease away into peace.

Long, long ago
she had odors of sweet perfume
of old man's cologne
we settled down for sleep
in a rhino bucket den
can this be overcome, he asks
can it be evolved
take your telephone
and dial it somewhere
doesn't matter whom
cannot wait to escape
cannot wish to fly
legends of blinds drawn
doors shut to the outside
sounds so dim they lie
presented to the spectrum
services now incapacitated
I'm dialing so far from home it hurts
and bad with biting language
worse than the sticks and the stones
a long glance from separate rooms
and now I lay down in the woods and wait to immerge.

A tale of thieves
of liars
of beggars
and the collapse of humanity
as little as we know of it
the children all stare into the wishing well
this is the story of the uninspired pair
who suffered miserably
setback after setback

Here beside you
I run like children with wings
I call names to the air
I sleep and walk in circles

I once went
under your skin
I looked in you
for a place to hide
I looked
for your sanctuary
within you, under
the place I could run
in you I hide
outside you where was I
I'm within you
my place is you

I feel sick
sit and wait
as the flies buzz my head
the heat and sweat just won't go away
it is night, I think, maybe
if it were I'd still be hot
but I could at least run and play
here I find a cold spot
and suddenly it is a dry sweat
I'm sure I'd give someone a fright
when in the middle of the night
they walk into the bathroom to pee
and instead of a toilet
they see me!
It's not much better outside
the bugs and insects are feeding on my open flesh
I'm a huge meal for them
here under the tree
I guess I'll go back to bed
and toss and turn in this intolerable heat
but I'll be damned this is the place I will lay
when coming through my curtains
is a new day!

In the land of the unwell
beasts wither and crawl
in agitation of their supper
that is the breeding grounds of the Devil inside
we strike out into the nighttime
like a pair of the dirty old dead
we walk near edges of ponds
this is home for us, the cool shimmering pools
I care not for the sounds we hear
nor the pitter patter of the unborn who can't sleep
it stretches days to weeks and years into life
we sit, lecherous beasts that growl,
prowling
and we hunt with razor sharp eyes
tigers amongst kittens
in heat
bugger off!
I can't remember
where I was.

You are hardcore
you are magic in my dreams
I strain to hear you
a faceless whisper
I care not for walking alone
or the prospect of an empty house
I dread the horror of the things
I'll never share
and when I find beauty even in surprising places
I will shake and tremble and quiver with you.

I walk the halls
and I see them
the sound of feet inside booths
soft porn
growing on the walls.
I broke it open
out poured the intestines
the guts and the fetus
of the piñata
the dizzying sounds vibrate my head
pounding and pulsating and beating away
it echoes like a trapped fluorescent light
and I see them again
a dead coyote springing forth to life
moving eyes of a mannequin with fingers
grabbing for my arm
I stumble on the front steps
and let the piñata shower upon us.

Does the forest beckon you
for just one more try
dwelling, swollen in fat caves
his written name crucified on a pedestal
the knuckles are crushed and spread wide open
some things beg earnestly to be nestled back
into bed
and lulled by a darkening coma
numbed senseless
green emerald shuttering light
she presents herself in the form of The Mother
so much wisdom, more a smashed tooth between
molars or a carcass mummy wedged upside down
The Mother has pain generating fingers and
instead of laughs she teaches the
fear of separating
why then, when we fall, must preaching and begging
and careless neglect
be the answer
and it never does seem to reply
reaction quick as silver steel
timing is key, timing is everywhere.

It was a season to love
a summer of hopes
and a place to fall out
where did it go
why did it leave so fast
is it time to go home
and search for our monkeys
lost vision and dreams
of a summer beach
and a tall lost girl
want to make her weep
look at how time flies
summer went away
won't return for long

This one is for the masses
making it big as a name
in the movies
I just wish he had been taught humility
teacher slipped a knife in the back
the answers stay the same
in an ever changing world
freedom is the smell
and the rhyme and reason just between you and me
the pigs at the farm were weaned
there is meaning in taking action
I robbed a dime and a nickel at full face value
donned a pair of flimsy sunglasses for a country romp
come home in those same old socks
and a gray overcoat
she said I was her in a strange sort of way
so I spilled out years of sordid stories.

The hidden meanings in their eyes
the superficial vision
make us look and smile
we saluted you back with the tip of our cap
and a raised glass of wild wine
the plastic alien day of the advertising age
comes across in yellowed, fragile pictures
you, the wild rebel creator
and the flamboyant one who we will always see
flashy pink letters and a woman keeping
abreast of modern times
while managing to age well
words get stirred in the pot
sometimes they come out in an untimely and depressing manner
the clock says no hurry
let it spin another hour or more
the days of paths to conquer
one of these times I swear I'll flip the page
but until then
keep on inviting the blues
for such a sweet touch victory
is best shared by two.

It eats you while you are sleeping
a slithering tail made of molten tongue
it could hurt you worse than
money. Perhaps.
Where does it sing
goodbye and good luck
hardly what I would call an end to
eleven years of 13
desperately she was forced to flee
when stinkweed's kilt revealed an enigma
why were you so complex
rock and roll never felt this good
in the southern states
the whole crazy circus reached its anniversary
and in memory, his grave stone
lost deep in vegetation and foliage
of a lonely little solider in fortune
shake this up
we can wait and imagine
about penetration in the morning.

He won't take it just anymore
felt the danger of its blow
why must you continue to ignore
drain the sorrowed sun
his own gladness
still makes us number one
the politics in the air simply disappear
delighted in knowing he is done
ran cowering to papa in fear
spends the rest of his life on the run
this one feels the love I grew
planted seeds of many paints
I just don't think you really knew
the number of virgin saints
a pocket full of lint
awoke at night clothed and very mad
his distinguished career marred by a dent
this is what is said.

The lady of the night flight
is induced into serene portraits
of a hopeless visionary saturated by the mark of plain troops
his face is masked with sweat as hands quiver
so close to her naked breast
hope becomes a serene mortuary
he writes his weekly letter to the clergyman
to sanitize unpardoned sins
castle in the air
dreamers and romanticists will fantasize as long as
breath channels through the body.

We decided to leave this one untitled just for you
a special resting place somewhere to call your own
it is with regret the picnic cannot be met
there were too many who were busy and others
just did not care
allow me to sit you down
steal this quick kiss and a fix
so this one goes untitled and it goes out to us
for once again some nearby night
no person will dare step in.

The bulb had been dimmed
until it was orange
and the reflection bronzed off the light
was caught on a rustic revolving fan
thin wisps of chilly air bounced down
and struck the linoleum floor
warm feet naked
shivered upon touching ground

Swans all lined up in a row
phony clown spreads himself to an audience
a final roar of applause as long as the hail keeps hitting
my skylight
fingers frail and skin torn loose
the bakers, they shove another pastry into the oven
their sirens sound night and day
glorified, a tornado of productivity
retrospective hallways
the man's goose clock sits perched on a spoiled oak slab
the tenants are the followers
of a brand new nation
they were forced to stop experimenting
with the lower caste ones
we've hatched what we can call an optimist
we'll trust them as the year progresses.

I've walked the cobbled street under moons
through gates of rainbow pasts
kept the summer leaves that have come and gone
and swept away
leaning hard against the window
green coated plastered rolling hills
blackened trees
light the sky
and you cover your eyes
a morning of treasured youth
one not quite for the exquisite
mended hearts and severed limbs
bring back the old story
his frosted chill produces stares
I've landed in your graveyard work
and settled for the fee
you and I suffer more
I'm caught in a wave, out to dinner, candlelight

Dipped
sanded away
taken to sea
desperately
forced to flee

He says there is a rumor to his impassionate glory
windows glide open for a moment
winter red hot wind swept through
she complained bitterly until it stopped
separated by thick Vaseline plastered eyes
and inch wide glass
the children made sounds as they created snow angels
which were photographed
now she looks for them in the fall
seeing the brown orange leaves
raked in a pile
but nobody is there
until they march in unison to furious drums.

He was quiet
she wept
spent many a night
in a sticky hot house
with no glass in the window panes
she no longer hesitates.

The cobra
lied and cheated
and it betrayed what it had
to its feasting friends
home at the mountain base
the venomous reptile
shed its skin and shook and shrank
and prepared to dine
mightily once more
the victim
froze
knowing it had been prayed upon
it smelled the danger
felt the stalking presence
quickly, darting to the left
in a desperate escape, running
right for the killer's eager jaw.

Whispering aspens
mahogany garter belts
fond of twisting back
eclipsing shadows
bent frowns
rugged sorrow
foreign import
lines drawn for convenience
inhaled them in
bold and unforgiving
both satisfying and disgusting
stickers to cover a hole
which the rat got through
after shave
hints of pine
Christmas ornaments
lodged eternally
nightmare not forgotten
earliest memory, is it?
Overwhelming deja vu smells.

My broken dream will always haunt me
inflicted a brand of torture on such an untested stallion
at hangman's grove rests a forest of cemeteries kept waiting.

We sweated and stayed and waited for the day
to arrive
it overtook me and pushed
I hurt her like she instructed
the growing radiation pink of dawn
soaked my blinds
and I forced my head out
to witness a childbirth of nature
this labor of love
stands awkward upon my heart
I'm a growing restless man
who determines sleep when his needs hinge upon her
he learnt his lesson
we shared common ground and delighted in
seeing the new beginning and the cycle of the creation
here, at the limestone rocks and the virgin creek
he felt pride in his passion.

Celluloid droning
it couldn't sleep
what a wasteful dream
its treasure chest
filled with bygones
let them be, it said
the best was caged away
inside a bubbled cave and glassy rocks
it sweated and stank in the angry cell
weak vision was aided by
a glowing green bulb which teased it
at periods of the day he entered and
inflicted streaks of red sores upon its massive body
day in and day out he never ceased.
They were amused
he laughed and roared
in his one-sided scope
he brought down his lighting fast snake whip and
sent a shock through its system
the creature filling with raging blood right down to its madly fidgeting tail
the chains snapped suddenly and it wasn't quite sure what had happened
the man's smile vanished and he backed to the wall
it let out a hideous howl and lunged forward, pushing furiously
and eagerly.

His windows, his landlords
the gate keepers
the guards
met his destiny: a crazed, frazzled mind
filled with intent savage anger
seeking out those it wants to punish
a long list checked repeatedly
names are dropped, forgotten, & on occasion, broken hearts
a shredded life
as light rains hit hard
mixing with asphalt into gray chalk
and men chomp on soggy fags
a waitress returns to her street
once more worried
inside, her doors are locked and she feels secure
no time for bad dreams
smell of soft warm lamps in multitudes of hazy colors
stuck in the senses.
Five stairs blink at midnight
sun god
empty gas canisters
the wine is frozen
much to the dismay of a man
and he will stop at nothing
to find a hole or an entrance
it started at the caves
deep and far he went
cool, jagged walls of fossils and stalagmites
at times he wanted to see the moon
or hear a bird make noise, music
he stumbled upon a waterfall, splashing blue streaks of wet
medicine off echoing cavern walls
along the hollow corridors and eroding Indian paths
he drinks without sleeping
hands cupped to grab gulps
he undressed and wore the cloth of the Indian
drew figures and symbols upon the marble
then he was rescued
to his better judgment, he went with the saviors
and the shaman clown was left out again.

Blaqueheart

Sleep catches up to dragging eyelids with a ferocious eagerness
like a plague and a virus
sapping anything in the way
the lids surrender to
being droopy and I curse me
I lay head to pillow and bitter
feeling stomach hunger pains.

> Outside in the humidity
> auto tow truck drivers wait like vultures.

Creatures stir in erotic sensation
a swollen frozen face on a bed of embers
he sings drunk in a chamber of petrified souls
little children in the night
flying, souls squirming.
There are bodies restless
flying in the darkness
come now and come all
you will find yourself waiting
rise and feel sanctuary left and right
sweet little angels sipping on alcoholic straws
find the animals who represent the whole
we will conquer this and become united
pass on the smoke and inhale and share
& I will become a part of you, not afraid
or swayed with devastation or war
this is us this is our world and our eternity
you will become a fully functioning part of it
scream now
she shouts with enthusiasm for a buck naked monster
you heard it stirring in the basement
locked doors revealing doom
the privacy has become young
drifting souls of decadent, narcissistic lost children.

Trucks in hibernation
like mothers in the womb
freeways are living cemeteries.
Sometimes my state of mind
resembles an abandoned rest area
of some warped after-school special.

I eat blond bombshell mushrooms
& feel up and down and inside you
flesh wound bleeds for days
somehow the backroom murder wasn't meant for us
a phantasmagoria of deprived secrets
slept on a bed of nails
a catastrophe, brutal mistake
assembled and buried in clown meadows
crossing X, falling under Y
I washed myself in a room of nausea fetus
force feeding off the lips deprived of the mother
it is not quite clear
I pray that the sucker dies in his sleep
what... what is that she hears?
she, the swimming slut in drag
castrates her realistic visions
I can read a fake like she can screw
and I'm missing the real thing
devil church offers late confessions
we all fall soundly asleep
got a finger sucking on the socket
I feel her feeling me up
could burst or die or just fly
entering her is entering waste
I can see it falling in 3-D monster vision
like the sunsets retiring
and I slink away
slink in sand, slink.

Drifting
came back to pleasantly haunt us
like you never left
the magic so enchanting
brings a feeling unlike anything else
greater and perhaps more erotic
could it be, so long after the death
that you have grown stronger and more mortal.

He wasn't sure where he was going
hey
where are you?
he didn't know
and he didn't remember what to do
men in thin round
glasses capture the sound of Irish punk in jars
a sweltering sea of
confused pre-organic life
cooks on the ocean floor
awaiting their turn
and standing isolated in line,
is a dreaded, hated
circus mime, coughing and hacking
acting as a samurai
caked in lime.

On a grizzled white beard
vultures sit and wait
for their turn
feasting on the inevitable.

A windowless plantation
the home rots with infestation
a hybrid of mosquito and frogs
gorging on arms
a draft tosses aside
the curtains
the slaves
stare listlessly
waiting to be inside
hot summer lemonade
the children hide.

Only after midnight
he was surprised at the sight of the Mexicans
that were wrapped tightly around his chest
and how this would become the most uncommercial
aspect of his life
he truly set out to make something that was simple
and it got lost
deep yearning & yelping from the basement
we can hear the moans, the soft desires
they want to peer inside you

She ate but wasn't hungry
couldn't stop listening from the bed
masturbating furiously with her severed hand
while outside in the garage,
emitted growling and passion
the auto eroticism inside a Studebaker.
A dying gardener stops caring about his militant ways
the happy dancing couple from the carnival smear makeup across one
another's faces
we imported you from down south, probably Portugal
does it really matter

She tells him that everything is better red than dead
we heard her outside the window of her parents clutching a knife
and scratching her nails on the glass
while the bored couple madly fuck
muttering away in some kind of undiscovered foreign language
a language they created from a dream one July evening
she stares at her father as he takes the knife away from her
& then they lavish the drama queen with a belt until her left eye slips out of
its socket

And we will meet you there crowded around the fire, drunk with kerosene
awaiting the arrival of the united taxi.
begin now the repetition of the expired guitarist
swallowing gallons of cancerous milk fresh from the bottle
feeling the itch scratching underneath the skin
plucking hair between teeth
the ancient wise one, come now and stroke the magic cock

there is doom in the words that shut the gate to the garden
follow me inside it, this maze, this glorious feverish nightmare garden
look inside, see a dead body, or is that a decapitated tree swollen with knots of blood
hungry gorillas feast
the hungriest will survive and one day make a smile and climb out to join the taxi
before storms strike and fierce rain lust against the barns and spoil a fire and a murder.

II
The Grand Unified Theory of the Ball

Little Comet

Little comet came to school and died one day
It wiped the dust off its television screen and moaned and groaned
And instead of waking up the next day it never rose to see the velvet curtains
That little comet sulked and cried and multiplied and smelled of odors lost long ago
But he didn't smell it, he didn't even consider that a petrie dish was in his oven.
And then, he was greeted by the mother-earth goddess, and he ran quick because
he knew if he didn't he would lose something pretty valuable to his little comet shape.
You can't smoke in here! yelled the greasy chef from behind the counter of a 50's diner.
But I smoke naturally! he yelled back, biting into his greasy cheese burger and greasy fries and, accidentally, a bottle of pure grease.
Funny enough he didn't feel like sticking to the wall.

Oh comet, where are you? Someone said you're pretty common and easy to get in the sack. But that's a potato sack to you, the one with holes carved out for a sack race.
No don't tell me they're not Ore-Ida potatoes, because that's not right! All right? Now sit down and write!

Caution! The warning label stuck out like a glaring neon traffic signal standing tall over a highway. It made him delirious and dehydrated and determined to keep going. He would run if he had to, his little comet legs getting him swiftly to the finish line.
That's a drag race he's in, someone said. Shh! Don't tell him. It makes him happy. Why ruin a good thing?

The comet had run over a deer on the ride to town. He had seen it clear as day but only too late, when its eyes reflected off his high beams, it snorted, and dodged in front of him. He stopped to examine the carnage. Never mind the car, he thought, it's stolen anyway, but look at the deer!

He trembled and shuddered. It had splattered all over his hood, barely even resembling a deer because the legs and neck were twisted in perverted positions. The head beams shone forward with a light red haze over the gray brick top of the road. He stared at the yellow stripes and followed them until he could see no farther into the dark.

In town it was cold. Traffic lights sat dormant, never seeming to change for the
non-existent oncoming automobiles. A peculiar wind picked up and rattled the branches of roadside trees recklessly, some of them making obnoxious scraping sounds against metal barns and on windows. The scent of peat soil hung in a cloud over the town.

“There are no prokaryotes out here!” the comet screamed out as loud as his little lungs could.

It didn’t carry far.

VW Bug

I knew a girl from the cheese state
She was always late and quite irate
I staked my sobriety
Upon wishes and dreams

She cruises town in a yellow beetle
She drives a VW Bug
Yes she does
She drives a VW Bug
When she does fleas flee

The route we take is paved in gold
We take the one of fools
Days are short and nights are dark
Hers is a paradise I'll never see

She grazed and grazed on grass
Breath as sweet as a cigar
High as a loon
Safe as a cartoon
On wintry drives
Live slippery lives

She drives a VW Bug
A yellow not maroon VW Bug
and going nowhere fast
We're tripping and falling
And she keeps on swallowing
Acting as a love machine
Was the girl I knew
In the back of her BMW

Who says you're right
When they all say no
Doesn't it seem frightening
Oh yes it does
With her at the wheel
As she drives a VW Bug

Morning Time

The morning is fresh
the sun cracks over the mountain,
the streets are still and lonely
something is in my air.
I feel it, it woke me,
I stirred.
Before it was not there
now it is everywhere and within
I leave and it follows,
I sit and it stays.
A bath, a bagel
milk and a fresh scrambled new day.
The door is shut but the lock isn't.
I have swallowed parasites
and I'm king of the anthill in my house.
I love what I had and was denied.
The pillow was satin and the bed a mattress
my tongue grew sweet and sour
I went places without really seeing them.
I've conducted an orchestra
while living in my squalid Idaho mountain village.
It built and leaped
and before I knew it, a monster was free.
I feel the world evolving
I see it waking
don't let the monster in
no reason to fear
when you sleep think of me
Slumber this day and next
It's a mess but coming out a flower.
I see no need for you to disguise and hide from me.
I want you to peer inside.

Closet Mozart Fan

And he named himself Roger but quite preferred the name Susan. Rather a remarkable chap whose face was seen plastered on blue mural walls on top of graffiti so as not to deface him. He collected coat hangers both plastic and of the metal variety, but never hung them in fear the value would go down. He blew sounds through rolled up cardboard tubes and put it to dance music and called it Funky Town. He had a girlfriend Beatrix and she made sculptures out of sand but nobody saw them. He locked up that room. Some would say he worked better in the dark but he always had a hint of a tan. So maybe I'm wrong. He had a lot of money of course, but he washed people's car windows just for a thrill (wasn't very good at it). Not long after he was hired, he was fired. But he still had good hands. The man listened to Mozart in the morning and Zeppelin by bedtime. Even as he grew more famous, he never acted any other way, not peculiar not odd or transparent and long, so maybe he was thick. The people adored him if they ever saw him, except when he went for drinks and smokes. And hey, one time he said, today, I'm going be O.K. but said it without a grin.

Untitled

I kindle the cross
dark clouds appear from nowhere
I felt them coming in
and my vehicle treks to
an empty backyard lot
And we walk many planes and cross moss flowered hills
sometimes I think about you,
and hope that in time as the distance binds
that if TV still runs, I could sit and dream about war
Come out and rescue me today
I know you have it in you to play the game.

The drink is repetitive
It brings you back for more
The grip hurts you through and through
Beasts gather within the bowels
The free spirit won't go away
It is the fatal flaw.

Freeways

Lying awake hearing barks of dogs
The sun casts empty stairwell shadows
A cops badge tumbles to the floor
Today the house is a casket
The moon drips. Candle wax solar system.
The movie theater won't open
Picture show for the blind
Blood seeps like rainwater
Fire turns to chrome

11

Down the highway
We see cloud puffs off the mountain
Smoke burns from the factory
Ghosts and wizards hitchhike in search of a town called
Familiar
The cactus grow wild like sprouting teenage girls
Baby rabbits hide under a slide
Awaiting their mother
Who is lost somewhere.
Box, cyndrical
They're creating the freeways
To a new and better tomorrow.

Feral Children

Feral children
Scream and cry
But don't know why.

Lunch is a tearjerker
A mobile phone of the ages

Poems are just songs
With the music stripped away.

Moon children
Are partial eclipses
Half the human they long to be.

About Someone We Once Both Knew

All conceptions
are stored in luggage
in haunting
living off welfare and sardines
angel children sleep and glow
as though they are neon bulbs of an era built
yesteryear
awake now, because we haven't much time
we drove to the shore
to pilgrimage like
abandoned babies
discovering meaning
for our first time
I can't forget
cradled in your arms
your icy kiss lacking in affection
distance apart makes you seem ugly
only my need brings me close.
dreams tumble out in saltshakers
I'm on the solo road
looking to find home.

Civil War Squirrels

The squirrels charged the hill at dawn
stampeding to the cries of the bugle
and feverishly rampaging onward
their cheeks bulged with nuts
tails flapping in the breeze
"Give me liberty, or give me death,"
yelled the squirrel general to his men.
The south didn't stand a chance.
By dawn they had triumphed
and taken the bunker
they chattered away noisily,
drinking and gnawing on wood
long into the night
infamy was theirs.

Shaman Breakfast

In an alley
a spotted child quivers in terror
the poet sits in his chair
as he hammers nails through his hands all night
a weeping barmaid scorches herself on a neon beer sign
the local homeless pet, a favorite,
found mysterious missing its stomach

Thousands of tiny bite marks.
A toddler in her skirt delicately licks a lollipop
her pale, hollow sockets stare listlessly ahead
she knows what happened in the alley
she is a mute.

The Shaman awakens now
bleeding in his beard
caked eyes slowly open and close filled with crow feet
thousands of gnarled shapes and pockmarks
the Shaman, under a blue fluorescent bulb
recites his mantra as whispers slide from his soft lips.

The deity stirs & shakes
the ground rumbles
pity the angels who feel nothing
as they are trapped and slaughtered
under mounds of ash & soot.
A beautiful woman, the Shaman's wife
kneels, then keels over
the agony too great
her hair sunk below ground like roots in search of water
red coated toes pointing to the moon.

Candy

She lifted her skirt high above the winds and spread out her arms to see where it would carry her
She believed in children's stories and nursery rhymes and collected toys she never tired of playing with countless times
They can't find anyone alive who wasn't once touched by her presence
You have to admire a girl who didn't believe in herself, hated herself, cried for herself
And adored her friends
She sat on the edge of the bed and read stories that made her smile
She sang sweet songs
She was beautiful, stirring, and complex

Stupid Butcher

The corner butcher was carving meat
And he seemed to have a story to tell
so I pay $15 for steak and stopped to listen
He breathed heavily and wiped his brow
His curly moustache certainly made him look like a Guido.
He stopped to talk, looked at me
And left.

Beatnik Blues

The days drag
send me away.
Sometimes the happiest songs are the really depressing tunes
the ones that bum you right out
I'm talking sad soul and soft jazz
stuff so miserable that life is a case of the gout
I groove to those sad tunes
Turn them on real quiet, like in my car cause I'm embarrassed and drive slow
Then I sing along and smoke
until I'm low on gas. So many miles spent just to hear my tunes
I chill to the blues, I sink way down, just escape myself, dig.
Like a cracker fish, you know?
Only for a bit and then, time to go home.
Dig sad vibes from the speakers.
I love those tunes people, cause I can think about them
and get really, really blue
blue, like that new flavored soft drink ya know? Like yeah.. I'm whisking away
cause sad tunes don't hide misery
only for a moment or two can I hide in that wonderful realm.

Highway Motels

The Long Highway travels deep desolate lost forgotten dreams haunt its wayside. Remembered like tombs built of roads. Decaying. Motor hotels, neon flashing signs inviting you to curious shops. Giant billboards faded and parched on the sides of barns are haunting trips to the past. Malt shops and burger joints. Auto conversations go nowhere along the old highway. Once again the main road is packed full of fin shaped automobiles. The highway is off the beaten path. Men and women slip into sexual intercourse on avenues and streets that cars will never dream of traveling again. They listen to the Moonlight Serenade, realizing time is running out.

Cigar

Confused old men
Sit around in alcoholic sweaters
Beating their wives
Swilling cigar ash.

child. easily swayed. manipulated. he wants to be so thin that his wet feet won't leave imprints in the sand. meditates hours on end in perfect frozen bliss. ignores wisps of the flute pan and Turkish incense. missing father since eight. missing mother in bedroom.

Bottle of Booze

I hear the commotions in my head, chug chug a chug. Listen deep within. What's that you say, the chaos of the echoes in the chasms burn, burn what, foolish man. What say you to this, this venomous hate broiling up, so full of empty anger. It's so bad for your skin, gives you a complex, and you think, nah, I didn't have no problems before- was silly, I made 'em all up. But these, these ones are sillier then ever but now I'm all bent out of shape from them. Sometimes it keeps me thinking so much I'm up all night, then I think about them again so I sleep all day. I like to pretend a full night and a half in bed will just rid me of the errors but now I don't even get that hopeful anymore so I know when I wake up I'll feel dragged and it won't get a lick better the rest of my short day. I make a mockery of myself, a parody of going straight. I know I want that piece of limelight. I know it. Admit it.

Why am I at home when I go to somewhere like a clothing shop, and why do I get that kick when I shop at the Circle-K. What thrills could I get there, that I don't get anywhere else.

Reflections of a Sunday

Everywhere I go
I know you lied to me
And everything I say
Wasn't true to me
In a genuine moment of my clarity, I hoped for more then a sign that you'd come home with me
And now I'm bored clear out of my mind sitting here watching the clock tick by
And maybe I could understand why if I just knew what you had to say to me.
I'm outside of my mind, I'm crawling through my skin.
I'm a little unsatisfied since we're not going out tonight. I check for dead lines but this phone isn't fried.
Maybe I'll take a dive.

Gentlemanly Affections of a Dirty Old Man

Let me entertain you
let me be your shining sun tonight
we'll go, just the two of us
walking hand in hand
what a day I'll make for you
we'll take the bus or maybe go by train, anyway you cut it,
this'll be one hell of a day
I'll shower you with flowers
It's a small token of appreciation for all the things you do
midnight beckons and I'll order coffee or tea oh can't you see
I'll make it one hell
of a day for you and for me
yellow moon over the pumpernickel trees. Sparkling stars
twinkle overhead, they light up the path along the red carpet I
laid for you.
And you spit on it and crushed a pecan muffin with your heels.
Thanks a lot!

Happiness is a Warm Cat

I'm drinking alone, but I have enough drinks for 10 people.
I'll drink tonight so I can forget I am drinking. I'm clutching a glass of vermouth. Now it's all over the floor. Hello, vermouth!

I hope nobody comes over, it means sharing the liquor for two. I'll be slamming back night caps and I'll drink until 1. Last night was one hell of a fight. I see bottles on the floor. I wonder if I had guests. This drink has got my name on it. But so does that one, and that one as well, and they don't have my name right. Highballs at 6. Then I'll go buy some mix. Drinking alone is a privileged honor. It's so easy to use and it drives away friends. Soggy eyes mean sour days. I'm muddling about in bed. Wine is cheaper then gin. The only warm body I ever see is a cat.

Child of Pirates

A child of pirates and a midget from war
He's a third class Hercules who cranks it out
Pigeons walk all over children
But the babies haven't got any say.

Mothers are asking indecent proposals to the glee of their daughter's men.
A doctor makes house calls but not if one snores!
Grampa calls you a whippersnapper but the old guy only wears white tees.
Make room for an herbal remedy.
We don't care how it gets there just drink it from a cherry tree.
A frog can be a wizard if he's allowed to be. That would be a sight to see!
My blood is untangled my arteries are free, it's clinically proven to make your head feel alive.
Wow stop me what a bargain at just 19.95. Little doggies are driving for the need to compete.
You can name a brown dog Blue and he'll still come running back to you.
Little child in a sandbox with a shovel loves to play. He'll grow up to smoke a bong but for now he'll be digging his way to Hong Kong.
What's the science behind this technology, with those screaming wild mad dog nukes following grandma home?
It's like a song, a melody.
A little slow, a little fast, a little bit fresh and new. At long last.
Purple fog
Nutty bed sheets
Twisted wind
Kinky divers
Mutts on the mind lately?
Dead birds don't squawk
Tip toes twinkle nose how r' you today
Gee it's late, pa's quite irate
Shovel, sadist!
Ring a ding a ling
Maybe, I did.

The End of the Unknown

I'm a purple dictionary
that glows when kissed by rain
I'm a mortician singing ballads
while the nymphs make love in graves.
        You are a sweet human remain
a leftover in lieu of shelter
to steer away strangers who flood salmon colored air.
They will use fresh soft bones
to construct the huts
taut skin for the roof.
The underground subway is running kind of late
for a girl in handcuffs who
thinks about playing in pantyhose
after her folks put the dog to bed.
The shine off a girl's purple fingers
reflect discount tickets to a crazed brain.
Don't trust that institution of theater mongrel dogs
feel a morbid start in the making.
Revel in a beloved ancient child's book
of pyrotechnic Neo-Nazi Egyptians fondling the
penicillin crusted doomed youth.
        Clowns are flocking in spiral bound churches.
They have cow hide skin, you know.
The leader is full of pity and flakes away chunks of the moon
what was our here supposed to do
but he kept flying
yes he's flying
and plants become residue.

Bar Fleas

The night flies when I'm drugged up and being a sore bastard
waking up under barstools and not even baths make me clean.
I'm swimming in my head, I'm a jumble, like a jigsaw, my feet welded down.
Children giggle and some call me funny, when I'm doped up on thrills and I beg them for money.
It's a sad world when you can't realize who the hell you are because your nametag is at work and your wallets in some bar.
I have a girlfriend you know what I mean I know I love her but she's only fifteen.
I feel like today is everyday, this is good as it gets. I'm knee deep in filth and I've lost all my bets.
Sad sad so inevitably sad, it's the state of affairs that get in my way.
Time flies ever so rapid as my brain slows, as I function less and get more sullen, the vomit flows.

Fun Inside Barrels

Older, we're not. I want to be there. Nestled against your face. Thumbing through your hair.
Older me. It's the sign of the times. Give it a chance. Let me talk to you and listen to the lyrics of songs you made mine. You bring peace to my rocky world.
I could never repay you like you deserve. Older me.

What happened to the ravishing beauty queen. You know the one, so pretty and prim.

Asylum

The buns are moldy
the cats vomit stains smell worse
bloody feces wiped on the bed sheets
glasses of unsipped milk have curdled
flesh rots and stinks in the bathtub
magic clowns foam at the mouth
scouring rats nibble at helpless toes
electric chairs are for torture here, not death
warped ex-brain surgeons continue to study the art of pain
lobotomized little children roam cold empty rooms with no reason at all
static filled TV channels are turned on for the elderly
forcibly impregnated women toil away in cellars kept from the sun
old dirty masters take care of the women, tending to all their needs
The animals are locked up for beating
Tired exhausted and mentally deformed servants are savagely hit as they work
the electricity is off
the hot water no more
the clocks have all stopped
and with it,
all sense of time.

33: a Metaphor I Don't Understand Yet
(includes a dream about John F. Kennedy)

You enter Aisle 33
of the grocery store
an aisle so long and narrow
you can't see the end
but your cart gets stuck
and you become frustrated and are unable to move it
products on the shelves start falling
you turn to leave and can't see a way out
in an endless corridor of the shopping aisle 33

You are stuck there
you'll die in 33

Human Bait

How is a boy to feel the rain
When it's streaming down
Catching snowflakes on her tongue
And he's dreaming
The sky will open up
And come falling down to
Where he's sleeping like a doll
Go on throwing stones
Be a pretty thing
Your feet are
Hooves of mammals all running in place
Your mind is haunted with
Frozen images, and this boy is free
So let him be
He will not stray
Nowhere to go
Empty, open inside
Dress up and hide
I'm the fish
I'm the flyer
I'm the bait
Stuck in the wires.

Superstar

Was the cry in the middle of the night
Just a plea or a yell for more
They say yesterday comes too early
And tomorrow is a forgotten day
Nothing's ever going to be the same
Only you'll always remain inside
And through this delicate end
All I care about is you
You traveled very far
To become my Superstar

I've been staring out the window
And the only difference is
One left me hanging
And another one evolved
By the by with no alibi
Can pretend all was a lie
But the only thing that matters
Is now I've got you here
You're a very special one
The one who left the door ajar
You're my Superstar

No longer going to long
In search of playgrounds
Where imaginations rule
Just sitting back with my Superstar
My true Superstar.

Blaqueheart

Enter the cave
Dance the sheets
Find the road
Follow the road
You see blue
I bleed red

Shasta Girl

She is wild
A fiery Shasta
In a shallow grave
Teach me how
Lets learn, together
This endless life
Makes me cry
Cut my wound
Swallow the shame
Put this on
Wear the hat
Enchanted by souls
Murder the night.

Her: a story to be continued.

You claim to take direction from the earth
your assistance makes me vulnerable
in silence you hear from way back when
erase the memory of time
the dead enter and exit
Like faceless clowns burning at the cross.
I feel thousands of tiny fingers reaching to me from below.
Can you smell death…
Does it have a name
do you cry when he touches?
I was taken into this arena of life unwillingly
I've danced among names whom I will never know
she stares at me
a rabid woman in heat.
Her eyes fucking me.
My soul is erotic
climb on me, let's paint day glo.
You feel freedom on top
when you ride, baby, it's bliss
but you walk through layers
like a broken down muse.
Do you feel agony in your final gasp,
do you hurt when you come?
I know you do.

Monsters of Energy

Listen to them
to the monsters of energy
feel their heat.

Along boulevards I walk
in awake, desolate dreams
I choose the birth of the night
enter the wisdom &
the trance of the tribe.
By paper I believe in god
and I'm turned on by longing
I stare at the stars and
I can look beyond
and I see in her the beauty she holds
I know of the gold and the riches.
I sing by moonlight
and only in its reflection will I feel my peace.

Lets ignore the ignorance our
society provides
we'll walk out to the glory of the isolation
that only you and I subscribe.

We move along and live for the day
cold in summer
time with perceptions of the sun

The moon is out but nobody answers.

Untitled

Come on, when is the ride going to stop
Hop aboard
Step into the parlor,
He said with a dash of audacity
Won't you come inside…
Let's turn off the lights
And see what you're capable of
And what I'm made of.

Sofia Blue

Arizona Camels

Morticians on a journey
finding the march
a path of slaughtered goblins
dangle from the trees
blood soaked baboons
gnawing and fighting ferociously
Jerusalem baby sucks from the gully
the camels crawled weakly with hind legs
dragging themselves through scalding hot white sands
over shattered skulls and humps.
The camels from Blythe are outnumbered
a handful of them march in packs
looking onward, snorting, seeking nourishment
the Arizona camels
curled up on the basin as the sun sets
a mixture of milky white red veins splattering the horizon
the final camel rests his head on the sand
just out of reach from fresh cool water
it breathes the last of its life.
The Arizona camels are no more.

The Dentist Sent me a Birthday Card

This season did not seem complete
my birthday was unjust
it seemed this special year would be a repeat
of all my previous ones, yet another bust
I went home and ate marble cake
cried into my towel and opened a gift I bought for me
and watered the beautiful floral arrangement they got me at work
this was just another birthday to be
alone like usual eating my festive salami
and jerking off in front of the TV.
When I opened the mail I enjoyed all the spam
a sale on discount tires and free ice tea. Oh I must go!
and a five dollar check from grandma, that gave me thrills
there was lo and behold a letter from my dentist
I could hear my heart stop.
With careful precision I sliced it open with glee
finally there was something tonight to make me laugh
and there inside a greeting card, I could barely wait to see what it said
they wished me a very happy birthday, from the dental staff.
They remembered my special day after all
my greeting made me feel very meek
when out fell a reminder of my appointment
to have my tooth pulled next week.

Ernest Cafe

My fingertips dance on hot bright bulbs
That illuminate the stark simplicity of a café that's
on the road to nowhere.
Your behavior tonight was not an oversight
we've monitored you, and we know
what kind of a worshipper you were.
I see them dancing with goat children
the fire brimming from their eyes.
That is the only thing keeping you alive,
that schoolyard was giving him erections.
I'm going to slip away from here
In one final gasp
I see no need for waiting by the side of the road.
Digging hands idly into my pockets
Searching for holes
waiting for some big moment to arrive
or for the earth to swallow me whole.
As the sand drips through my toes
heart beats still like a dying echo,
as it dances down the corridor.
My friends, we've entered the final ball
the arena that says farewell
without repent, with no regret, you don't turn back.

This is the destination,
The game you always yearned to play on hot sweaty
summer days.
Retire now into the embers of sleep
Close those charcoal colored eyes
And find your inner dream
For you won't rise
And nobody will see if you stirred.
Sleep, endless sleep.
Sleep.
Sleep.

Banana Pants Don't Make a Man

Filthy lines of chalk cover sidewalks on every corner
The treasure is underground, you see
Each day looks whiter, but
every following year just brings more wretched "Christmas Carol" movies for TV.
Damn you, Scrooge!
The hurt is deep and love won't keep
I'd rather die in silent nights than
Lose face and say goodbye.
So many feel alive during blissful slumbers under the pecan tree.
It's like a little sunshine filtering through your blond hair
And coughing blood on dry sidewalks until it cakes.
I kissed mirrors when I had fear
And still I'm alone, but crying like a beast.
Stare, look and you'll see me as I want you to
You'd never know what I am on the outer realm. But I enjoy pie more than cake.
I'm afraid & I lie to you,
I lie and I walk alone
I thought I found myself at the garden springs one day.
Inside my eyes, crawling to safety, closing off this stranger's land
I almost freed the inner horrors
But it went lost. And now they're putting my life story out on DVD.
The fires made us insane
We waited for the fall to roll around
& I thought I'd make it all good
But the mines have collapsed and gone inward
They fell apart and we rode home.
I'm tucked away.
Screaming.
Shine, shiny, kiss and try to understand
Banana pants don't make a man.
Fly but never raise an inch.

Smoggy Japanese Nights

Sphinx burial is a sexy death
it is your notion to spin
I could not help overhearing
the previous conversation
What did I miss and where did it start?
I wish you were not a liar
Slipped away in the night, this is what he did
Pour some tea and listen to the story
He slipped away,
never said a word, and went east
Whiskey poured over warm ice.
Leaving thin streams reminiscent of flour.
They say a lot....
I was hounded for a body
Not matter, nor a brain
Everything is strange during storms
I once caught my reflection
In a Japanese mirror
I can't help questioning a million things
Having yet to receive an answer
Try remembering your middle name.

The Frown

If I don't make it back
keep the buns in the oven.
He was a child protégé
fell off the trampoline
and his dad said
"Go get the mail."
So he went outside
and walked to the mall
but they wouldn't let him in
because he was too small!
Frowns.
They're all around.

Summer Zombie Movies

Corpses run amok
everything has gone too far
they're crawling from the sewers
you can see them peering out of manholes

Billy the Kid's gang can't defend themselves in this cowboy world gone wrong.

This is a sick sad demented forest where a man can get a beer but he can also have his blood drained by a witch who looks like a mermaid dripping in rat shit inside a psychedelic western saloon at dawn in winter.

They go home then, when the light finally penetrates rhythmically flashing bulbs violently, striking and beating the walls and the roofs harshly. Even during a walk with the living, we'll have to shield eyes from the fright. Oh the horror of this awakening hour. Put me back to bed with a bullet in the nightstand and hot tea.

Can you film the silver that is shaved off the metal lining, so we can turn it into a motion picture seen only by two?

Chinese lanterns dangle precariously off pagoda shingles.
It is murder to not light them and leave it so dark your mate cries in fear.

Fires burn inside barrels.
Rats sing in carols.
Helmets mash together

Books turn into pages to identify new chapters in a best selling novella they're writing within the inner-core of a complex new technology that has allowed the pulp to become alive and think and function like the human brain.

One day there will be computers seeking laughter on planet earth.

They learn without reasoning

We have to admire them
Do you want the alternate evil rule, instead? the audio-visual asks as it sharpens its tools in a hot shed

I bang the floor because that is when I learned to crawl
I entered the socket. Its holes accept me
mascara drips into my mouth.
On a crisp, somber day
your laughter is sickening
I see your white fangs
you can take me, I'm vulnerable. What are you waiting for?

The Hobo

No weather could keep her down
beautiful peach
she was a well wisher
gorgeous in the reflection
laughed among laurel trees
gasping for tears
knowing there was a price to her happiness
on the last night a fly lights up
the empty creek could gurgle- with a little help.
Misery makes her grin seem goofy
she handles herself so delicately like a wasp enjoying honey from a flower
what a pretty girl, so sappy, with glee
she has gone fanatical with cheerful cries
you could hear her from across the yard
wishing for a personal picnic
with tea served right from the brook and water boiled out of the ice.
The little boy shimmied himself down from the tree with his hobo bag and a bunch of bananas
he made it to one end of the block before the smell of oregano and tomato soup brought him back
sounds of drummers from the giant glass door
behind it the cake with He-Man on it
he hangs from his knees
and the girls laugh
his shirt hangs over his face but his dopey grin is wide
he stands over the parents and jumps on their mattress
forever the orange blanket sits over colossal windows
peering over the square
they hand him a penny and he pushes it away
We'll always be here for you.. they say.
he swallows it.
The hobo strikes back out to the field
he sees corn and meadows and marshes and brooks and trout
his great stick, his hobo kit, held firmly in hand
I'll hold onto you forever... he says.
He never looks back and peers forward

they laugh behind him as his bare feet forge ahead
he swats at mosquitoes and the fence draws near
the fruit looks unappealing
streets are flooding with water
who cares if it never rained
or if the hydrants hosed it down
for these moments he will always be in a boat
steering, not letting the crew down.
Found a shotgun in the closet yet stayed silent
went knee deep into the water and saw palm trees gushing by
and there she sat on the top bunk, waiting
the clam shell night light flashing across super hero blankets
he refused to eat the spinach anyway. But they promised him strength.
Warmth was finally created
all the memories were wasted in time and blended
cut in rows
haircuts inside barns brewed with jellies & jams on shelves
curled locks saved inside envelopes
this quiet creator of his life
I saw smiles on their faces
pressing against the slime covered windows
in the distance the old man mowed grass
swiping at fireflies as they glowed and blazed
and all the heads turned and watched
as the car angled
pulling into the driveway
the little boy scooting past on his cycle
the little girl dreading another move, hiding in the living room behind the lava lamp
wanting to go away
and these were all the things he would see gaze by in the years to come
as he bought a soda in the grocer
admiring the abandoned cars rotting in the overgrowth of trees

I told you.
I love you so.

The Pizza Man

The pizza man is molesting
his teenage ham and pineapple pizza pie
along a dark and deserted street that no sane soul dares breathe on
a demented queer fairy in a Santa outfit stumbles and staggers ahead
he reaches into his sack of goodies and
pulls out his cock
decorated with a wreath and jingling tiny bells
a small car with pizza lights
blazed in neon, pulls to the corner
it backs up, turns, and eventually drives away

The Madness I See in You

Green suited monkeys
turn into nilhists
creamed colored golden flowers
blood soaked nutmeg
they are up for a challenge
diving off seven story balconies
into dry pools of cracked concrete
angry hooded monks huddle in bitter silence
desert tumbleweeds mingling in
group orgies, groping and sniveling like catty wives
confederate glass eyed soldiers
march in monotone steps forward
drums suspended from zero gravity rotate
pilots suck thumbs as tourists travel
shoe salesmen dance with armless soldiers
the women in the park all castrate a dove
while pigeons drink tea and stimulate their genitals
tin cans rain down and blossom into oranges
fertilizer in the mind
a faceless doctor amputates away
his fingerprints
are erotic billboards
sucking out neon with his teeth
feel them vibrating, feel them creating the body
metal signs glowing an amber hue
veins sprouting up and down
its shiny glossy hand
blood circulating, eagerly filling it
the metal nilhist agitates its brain
he has an itch he cannot reach
jammed pencil in the skull
eye socket bulging, mouth collapsing
saber toothed blink.

Crusty Sea Men

Women dance naked
upon pirate ships
a feast of souls
aboard the rotting war ship
hair sparkles gold
in spite of the light
they jump from deck to deck
bosoms protruding
splattered with sea salt
crusty iron swords
gorged in the hulls
out forward in sea
floating backward
drinking Chamomile tea
blood bath happy.

Seasonal Changes

Porcupine refried dogs
plastic explosives
sweat falls down the chest of
a fairy tale maiden
letting her hair down to
invent a fable
bubble soaked
semen leaks over
the maiden
she orgasms
in successive tidal waves
seeds are amazing
fertilizing & swelling
mutating, expanding, passing genes
lovers like corn, planted
with soft fertile soil to
harvest seasonal changes
crops are giving birth
where once was eager ground
now plowed with fruition of
mindful young greenery
the tips full of stalks
soon to drop seeds
a farm of incestuous growth.

Gone West

Window glass panes
cry of the church stain
rows of praising chairs
felt ungodly
they know
going west, going with nothing
just knowledge of a better land
not the son of a bitch she left behind
I see the lonesome cougar
a restful one
log cabins and cutting wood
old sawmills filled with black lung and jolly
workers
plastered.

Child of Christmas

Merry Christmas child
I hope you know who you are
and where you began
if that's the case you are the only one
your future is bright
and the stars above you look right
to be on your merry little way
but don't count your blessings quite yet
because a mirage is never here to stay
merry Christmas child
your wandering blue eyes look curiously around
for every moment is a new beginning
everything so uncertain for you, little boy
but you smile like you sparkle and you never frown
the winter trees are green and so clean cut
like they're frosted with powdered snow but still standing tall.
The carolers sing hearts out and you know it won't be long
before they're coming to our driveway

Hey, merry Christmas boy
this is your journey
take the gifts and run
you decide where to go and where to play
look inside yourself and learn who you are
climb out of bed, so warm and cozy in those cotton threads
run down the stairs
hug your mum and dad and see what presents lay under the tree
on this Christmas day.

Weasel Sandwiches

You are like a weasel in the night
scampering over trash outside my window
the face of pockmarked weasel's irks me
as though a quail of serenity was shoving yellow tailed ducks
into a fan
can you see the feathers of their lust, shooting out into the air?
or the splatter of their intestines, gluing themselves to the ceiling?
oh, odorous weasel, I yearn for you
come sniff outside my window
let us strain on our hind toes and nibble on peanuts at the ledge
a hat on my head is like an analogy for licking canned yams
from the freezer.
we are not un-alike, you and me
weasel
we both need a shave.
and we stink of last night's pail pink bourbon.

The Hamsters

Everyone was dead
and the floorboards creaked a bit
probably letting off some steam as the gases rose and left
at first only a few dwarf hamsters emerged.
Tiny pink noses peaked out in search of the light
but they were so blind and hungry they went for the meat
the nearby swimming pool quickly became a haven
for kamikaze hamsters belly flopping away
one stood out in the sun
his belly basking in the blood red sun
he nibbles the meat from his whiskers and found a wheel in which to run.
It is Hamster Day, finally, the hamsters declared with eyes bulging
there could not have been better planning, the arrogant humans were at last put to bay
the dwarf hamsters emerged confident, meat in their teeth, swords drawn
if there were any human survivors, they had little time left,
the hamsters were ready to play.

Captain Bubbles

Captain Bubbles
from beyond the deep sea
Captain Bubbles
delicious suave and calm
Captain Bubbles
he has come to see you free
Captain Bubbles
a man of his honor and word
Captain Bubbles
he kills then stops to study the Psalm
Captain Bubbles
he made his bed with the feathers of a dove
Oh yes Captain Bubbles
The fabulous Captain Bubbles
He is everything a spy should be
Dry vodka, a cigarette and woman make three
He smokes
he steers a boat
he loves you gingerly
Oh Captain Bubbles
A total gent
let us hope it never gets out
that he serves his people faithfully
and is only a lowly sergeant
Captain Bubbles
We adore him anyway.

Infectious Bathtub

There are smiles and grace
blessing your ugly face
bloodied baboons tear into each other
with a furious pace
shredding limbs apart like clots of paint on ink brushes
pulsing screaming grey matters of pulp pushed together beating rapidly
madly pulsating beating in tune to rapid hearts
brains melting seeping into pours tunneling through
manholes
finding their way into the big ditch
empty go carts sail through the great race
filled with vessels of human skulls, their minds grinning, tangling together
as weeds
clamoring in and around one another
individual smiles crooked eyes bent and slant half closed with no sleep
he has not rested in a year
he does not want to slow down
he wants to stop, alto, at Pinos Altos.
does not want to see things on the floor that are not there
& not want to walk the room and see the living breathing corpse of his dead
mother
rocking in a chair that was never supposed to have been bought, not this
young an age anyway.
he sees the crawling creatures and figures in the corners of his eyes making
spider webs
he jumps, he freaks
people did not understand even when he did not see the things, when he did
not think
there were worms crawling from the tan carpet
or the day the flesh colored half inch beast in the lake where he waded
would crawl into a small cut on his foot from where it lived on a rock
covered with moss
he watched it, he watched it! before his very eyes, as it slipped inside
the pink bloody hole
an analogy at that age he would not ever understand
at eleven but even as a boy
the holes in his clothes became vicious enemies attacking his body
trying to find a way to tunnel to his pores, to his toes, to his feet, to the

exposed openness his fragile skeletal structure offered to the viruses
he cowered and withdrew at night in the horrific sanctuary of blackness to the bottom of a blanket that had a tail end wanting to wiggle within
he saw crevices, holes, pits in the shirts and pants and pillows
everything seemed against him but he was stupid and incredibly insane
he would not reasonably stay awake for hours blinking eyes to the clock on the mural
how soundly the imprint of the 12:00 in red burns in his retinas to this day as his eyelids sank and shut and open to perfect synchronization to match it
his fingers drumming surfaces in patterns he would never explain but kept the family alive
he shudders and squirms and sickens at porcelain, at the mere hint of the rounded surfaces that infect and crawl and attach their micro bug claws into his hairs and cling
they won't wash away
he stands before the bathtub wanting to be ill, just from staring at the water. He sees no reflection, he would vomit crawling into that tub of infection
get in, they won't hurt you
getting in. Oh no.
Swarming like a herd of locust with melting stingers to slide and slip between crevices and burrow away within the selected parts of who he is
he is only a physical human body anyway, within that exists no soul, no personality, simply an empty vessel of bodily organs and something hiding in his foot
the rust spots at the bottom scrape and dig and massage with devilish tingling fingers
enter him, now.
sludge... he will forever through the rest of his biological breathing life, carry insects of which none shall ever be explained or studied in any scientific journal
even at two decades later
grin and bear it, the bath is clean
soap, clean and have a good scrub up
crying, hurt, fearing the night.
Fearing the hand of some unknown freaky sadistic saint to torture and mutilate the two in the next room
would I feel them near as I grew old?
suppose the next day there was stillness from their bed
if I stopped blinking, if I did not do as I was told by these forces
would I see them even make the next snow covered morning?

Pill Farmers

People are taking horse pills
in an effort to fix themselves
they are diseased in the mind
rotting to the core
little sickly bunny rabbits lodged away in the brain
looking forward to extermination
they have to swallow the powder
waiting for the trip, they wait, and nothing happens
and suddenly the powder hits and they wish they were dead
they have another three hours of tripping before they won't care
bugs are running around the floors and people are trying to crush them
it is a futile effort, so we hand them more powder and they inhale it
pretty funny watching those bastards scramble around for roaches in the
wood
soon there is so much powder everywhere that they are dry humping the
stuff
getting it smeared into their pores
one of them drew a steam bath and dumped the shit all over hot coals
I had little sympathy for his addictions and I thought about pushing him onto
the rocks
but that dumb weasel sat down in an attempt to pop one off
we spent the rest of the night fixing burn marks on his asshole
with burns like that, it looked like he'd been kissed by a Coleman grill.
and if you gazed a bit deeper, a French kiss.
For a little while I thought I was a cougar and I was living free.
Beautiful. Surrounded by wild cougars.
until the damn things shrink wrapped and morphed into goddamn wood logs
floating up stream.
this was a time for freaking and I had plenty of it.
hush over the ridge, I want to jump into a sunset and eat it like an enchilada.

Harvest of the Scarecrows

The harvesting had begun and the meadow was full of scarecrows
two farmers, a father and his boy, dreading the summer heat,
set to work
sun scorched down and burned all over their farm, heating the crops
torching the eager and hungry fertile ground

They worked mightily, plowing their giant earth machines
across the soil
preparing for the new year, for the new harvest
the dirt moaned and tumbled underneath the heavy chrome blades
spurting and splattering left and right and ahead
and behind them, the scarecrows stood spooking off the wild beasts in
the air

It was then that one of the scarecrows, a straw hat sheltering the face
made of an oat bag
twitched a finger
one by one, the gloved hands stirred as the rumbling of the ground
from the machines
disrupted its slumber
feet, planted solidly into the moist earth, unhooked themselves from
the wood pole holding it vertically
a button eye twitched, a stir of recognition
the scarecrow stepped one foot forward, sinking in
and then another
soft crunching in the ground and recognition in the listless eyes

The men on the machines wiped moisture off faces and grubby hands
sweat mixing into the soil
the feet of scarecrows softly trailing behind them
smelling the trail of the men's sweat
one after the other they came
finding the ability to move, sinewy muscles of straw and yarn.
The father, pleased with his work, shut down his machine to drink his
cool water
he swallowed, his neck straining, waiting for his son to follow behind
the dusk was setting in and it was nearing time to leave
he looked back for his boy, and gasped. The bottle dropped from his

hand.
He watched the scarecrows grabbing his boy, pulling him from
the earth machine. The boy struggled for a while as they
smothered him
one after the other, scarecrows climbing on him, mounting him
their clothed bodies smeared him, wrestling and pushing against him
in feverish gluttony
they worked him into the ground as though planting him
a seed in the farm
the boy's fingers stretched to the sky, yelping, then nothing.
The farmer gasped as he felt something on his shoulder
he turned to see a gloved hand gripping him, almost questioning
his presence
then it pulled him from his seat

The harvest had begun.

Futuro

I found heaven today
I'm agnostic
so that's a lot to say
the Swedes created divinity
this is paradise, the last hope of getting away
during the harvesting the UFOS sought refuge
within dozens of tiny oval holes.

I am Nobody

Who are you?
I'm nobody.
What do you mean, you are nobody?
I am nobody.
That is ridiculous. Everybody is somebody, fool.
Well, I am not.
Yeah you are. I see you.
Good for your eyesight.
So, who are you?
Nobody.
Look, I'm somebody. And I know you are too.
Good for your faith in humanity.
This is silly. Tell me who you are.
Go away.
Look, I have a name.
Lucky you.
So what is yours? I'm Jim.
I'm not interested.
I'm not selling anything.
Then go away.
I just want to know who you are.
I'm nobody, I have no self.
Yes, you do. You're talking to me, you obviously have a self.
(silence)
Yes I am somebody.
Great. Who?
I'm somebody who is annoyed by you.
Oh, go to hell.

Sketching Memories

A ridiculous child nursery tune won't slow down
as the phonograph skips and echoes
despite the wet stains of the boy who drooled a spot in the middle
he can hear it in the background
over a bowl of tomato soup that stains his collar bright red
if we go around once more, another mile, our lungs will explode
hides behind a wall plastered of stone, he grabs a hose
and sprays the middle rock
he lives out his fantasy of being a superhero
by seeing himself escape from the garbage chute
we went there once
across the pond filled with green lily pads
skipping frogs and stones
he tried to take home a piece of it all and had it blown back in his face
threw his rock away and never found it again
gazed at the stars
she kissed me then
or so I thought, it seemed like the thing to do
it felt right but she ran off and the blanket was washed away from the
sand
she ran into some cabana and I made a raid for the water cooler
I didn't follow her again and we lost track and that was alright
stayed home sketching paintings of the last sand castle ever built
and there was no doubt, sticks of caramel for dinner
little fat school girls paint telescopes and binoculars in science class
will be days before their teacher screams and yells as he tries to gaze
at the distant planets
for the very first time, he wakes up on the couch and watches a fly
buzz around his private parts
doesn't know why but he loves running around in his underwear
some night later a brick would smash the window
and he went jumping off a log into a creek

or was it just a meadow overfilled with stale rain
forever he sits in the top bunk of a children's bedroom with the lights turned low
and the hideous glow of the night light that he hopes will burn out, and yet hopes won't go away
makes a horrible smell as it burns and pops in the socket
then at night he visions the house burning up, sparking from a sweet smelling match
blurry from sickness his eyes cannot focus as the bonfire outside his bedroom window
takes place and dozens of strangers dance and yell and break bottles
in the morning he will awake and find them passed out, faces pink from too much sun and too much fire
he thinks maybe they just need water when across the street the wooden gate closes shut
the iron wheels grinding and slamming for good
they'll spend a restless night looking for the dog that ran away in the snow
footprints all the way to an alley before they vanish into the creek and there are
angry bums cussing and chewing on wine bottles
the dog shows up, probably hid in a manhole, appears in the garden where I stand
as gum dissolves into liquid in my mouth and I spit it out, but it never really goes away
he smashes the bricks and stone into the wall to eliminate the wasps
he fancies himself a ghost buster
and again that night he saw the school as it burned and burned like bushes from firecrackers
and he could see
the charred walls and the water fountains toasted by blackness
I run down the street trying to make it into the air
dog hairs flying off my shirt
and keep running faster and jump a little
then finally, at last, I take flight
and I fly a little bit, ecstatic to make it at long last
I go forward a bit until I come back to the ground in a full run.
And he gave himself to hell.

The Solarium

The cool breath of alcohol, a harsh, stinging toxic reliever, has been a preoccupation with man for hundreds of years. In the late portion of the 1990s existed a bar within the city of Tucson called Solarium. Its ambience, that of water green plants, tables on rise lofts over metal ramps, and soft jazz wafting from a grand piano, made it seem high class to these eyes. As classy as could be in this town. And indeed, it was. A drink at Solarium was akin to blissfully feeling you were swept away into a tropical club somewhere in the Bahamas perhaps, capping off an evening with strong drink, good company and service that respected and catered to you. Every worry vanished away. It was a place of tranquility and kindness and escape, the sort of retreat that two gentleman needed to escape the harsh reality of life in a strange and unsettling time.

Tucson, it seems, was not this place.

Blaqueheart

The Last Beach

At evening's shade we walked out to the beach on a full moon night and hiked along into the sandy wet turf a ways until we found privacy.

"Could be the only ones alive out here," she said, her dress blowing in the light breeze.

We walked a little further to give ourselves a chill and to wash off the sand that had collected between our toes.

My feet rested beside her, and it was nobody but us and whatever we made of our time.

We spread out a blanket and looked at star patterns. Out here alone the two of us felt an aliveness that I hadn't felt in a long while. She sat between my legs
and stared out into the black ocean.

I smelled fragrance on her skin.

Not familiar smells of perfume and oils, but a wondrous scent of salty ocean sea.

We kissed, and my hands stroked her sand covered body. We both felt it then, and trembled slightly and I could see we had arrived.

She is Gone

There is a time of evening
the sun has gone milky white
grayed as a woman nearing her twilight years
if you look to that blank expressionless sky
and see pine needles in reach
hanging carelessly from swinging limbs
they sway, as though the tree has hundreds of restless fingers
and the solid pine tree stands firmly rooted
dripping cones
I watch the monochrome decaying backdrop
onsets of nightfall push in
branches flailing up, down...
the gravel beneath my feet crunch
soon it will be this color
and this day has set, for good. This is it
the exact moment, frozen in time
when I knew, when I realized
a thousand million branches stretched out into the sky blinding
my vision
it was an amazing setting sun with no rain
a helpless, lost day, unable to turn around time
the day when I knew she would be gone.
As the pine needles darkened
and fell off
they went brown, and crumbled
withering on the ground.

Lightning Bugs of Missouri

They call them lightning bugs up here
I always knew them as fireflies. But these little creatures light up like flickering candles in a soft wind.
Coming back here, to see the cuckoo clock at the hour to the ancient bottles of
Doctor Scholls (insert miracle cure here)

The train passes by, proudly tooting its horn. Crickets and locust, I presume, buzz by the window, disrupting my concentration.
I can recall catching those fireflies once long ago. She brings out a glass jar and we try to catch them now. They won't bite.
Swimming in the creek so many years ago seemed like the largest water in the world. Now it is a dry bed.
Playing hide and seek in the trees.
Running along the cracked sidewalk and chasing invisible foes with a scooter.
I wonder what she went through, living here, how far she had come, where she went.

I see little pieces of myself here.

Now I see a little bit more. I peer into the windows of the old garage, where I sat with a towel around my neck, waiting
for the dreaded haircut.

And she stands there once again.

And I know she will always be here no matter what happens, or where I go, what I say or do.
Now I wait for my time
watching the bugs fade away inside my jar until it grows dark
and the eyelids
close shut.

Jar

She gasps with a somber breath
final whispers
I want the trees and plants to be green again
I want the paint on the front porch to be bright red, the wear and tear gone
I want the punching bag back, her fists mashing its skin
taken her last breath
come get her.
she is here. An entire existence waiting to be packed up
with false and immodest hugs
blood seeps from snipped vines
I look in and see a human life, left on display
wanting to be alone, wanting them to go away
smothered by people crowding in to say goodbye
like she's a circus attraction
friends buying tickets for the show.
It won't escape you
formaldehyde.
Watching her sleeping from my chair
seeing her waking eyes gazing lovingly at me
and smiling with me.

Blaqueheart

About the Author

William Bevill resides and writes in Tucson, Arizona. He is 31.

Aside from publishing poetry, he is at work on several novels, plays, short stories, and a film. For more details:

Email: williambevill@gmail.com

www.myspace.com/drbenwayproductions

William Bevill

www.ingramcontent.com/pod-product-compliance
Lightning Source LLC
LaVergne TN
LVHW090952080826
845145LV00003B/981
* 9 7 8 0 6 1 5 1 5 0 3 7 6 *